Secrets of the Deep: The Mystery of the Loch Ness Monster

Edward Turner

Published by Oliver Lancaster, 2023.

SECRETS OF THE DEEP: THE MYSTERY OF THE LOCH NESS MONSTER

First edition. July 8, 2023.

ISBN: 979-8223778936

Written by Edward Turner.

Also by Edward Turner

Ghosts of Paris: Ten Haunted Places in the City of Love

Appalachian Nightmares: The Top 10 Creepy Creatures of the Mountains

Asia's Top Ten Cryptids: Legends, Sightings, and Theories

Beyond the Shadows: Unlocking the Mystery of Bigfoot

Evil Women in History: Uncovering the Gruesome Crimes of Ten Notorious Female Killers

Ghosts of London: Ten Haunted Places in The City

Ghosts of New York: Ten Haunted Places in The Big Apple

Ghosts of Oregon: The Top 10 Haunted Places You Must Visit

Ghosts of the Stage: Ten Hauntings at the Theatre

Missouri Nightmares: The Top 10 Chilling Legends

Mothman Unleashed: Into the Darkened Skies

North America's Top Ten Cryptids: Legends, Sightings, and Theories

Philly's Phantom Encounters: Exploring the City's Most Haunted Places

Secrets of the Deep: The Mystery of the Loch Ness Monster

Unsolved Mysteries: Delving into the Shadows of Infamous Murders and Enigmatic Killers

Unveiling the Shadows: A Journey into Financial Crimes and Scandals

Secrets of the Deep: The Mystery of the Loch Ness Monster

EDWARD TURNER

Introduction: Journey Into the Depths - Unlocking the Mystery of the Loch Ness Monster

In the heart of the Scottish Highlands, shrouded in mist and mystery, lies a body of water renowned as much for its breathtaking beauty as its most famous, yet elusive inhabitant. It's a lake that stretches like a darkened glass ribbon through the rugged landscape, its depths holding secrets whispered through centuries. This is Loch Ness, and the enigma that dwells in its depths needs no introduction. It is, of course, the Loch Ness Monster – Nessie to her countless fascinated followers.

"Secrets of the Deep: The Mystery of the Loch Ness Monster" is not just a book; it's an invitation, a golden ticket into a world teeming with folklore, science, scepticism, and speculation. We stand together on the brink of a journey into the unknown, armed with nothing more than our shared curiosity and a thirst for truth.

The Loch Ness Monster phenomenon is a fascinating tapestry woven from countless threads of history, mythology, biology, psychology, and sociology. It is an extraordinary blend of fact and fantasy, science and supposition, cold logic and wild imagination. But what makes this legend so captivating? Is it the mere idea of a prehistoric creature lurking undetected in our modern world, or is it something more profound – a universal human yearning for mystery, for a connection with the ancient and the unknown?

In this book, we will trace the origins of the Loch Ness Monster, from ancient Celtic folklore and early historical accounts to its enduring presence in popular culture. We will examine the tantalising scraps of evidence - eyewitness accounts, murky photographs, sonar contacts, and mysterious ripples on the water's surface.

We will delve into the minds of both believers and sceptics, exploring psychological phenomena like pareidolia and mass hysteria. We'll probe into the motivations behind hoaxes and the allure of cryptozoology, the study of hidden animals. And in our quest for understanding, we'll consider a host of potential explanations for Nessie, from surviving dinosaurs and giant eels to misidentified mundane phenomena.

Yet, this book is about more than just the search for a mysterious creature. It is about the human thirst for discovery and our relentless drive to explore the unknown. It's about our capacity for wonder and our willingness to question. It is, in essence, a tribute to human curiosity.

But be warned: as we embark on this journey, we may find more questions than answers. The secrets of Loch Ness run as deep as the loch itself, and each mystery unravelled often gives birth to another. But isn't that the essence of any true exploration?

So, come join us on this expedition into the depths of the unknown. Bring your sense of adventure, your openness to wonder, and your scepticism. Because in the search for the Loch

SECRETS OF THE DEEP: THE MYSTERY OF THE LOCH NESS MONSTER

Ness Monster, it's not just about finding answers. It's about learning to question, to explore, and to embrace the mystery.

Welcome to "Secrets of the Deep: The Mystery of the Loch Ness Monster". Our journey begins here...

Chapter 1: Legends and Lore

1.1 Ancient Whispers - The Roots of Myth and Legend

Long before the Loch Ness Monster's serpentine silhouette began sparking intrigue across the globe, the enigmatic waters of Loch Ness were a staple of Celtic and Scottish folklore. They hold stories that, to this day, linger as murmurs among the winds and ripples, carrying the weight of ancient tales and shadowy figures who were believed to inhabit their inky depths. Central to this ancient lore are the water spirits and mythical creatures, entities that carry a significant influence in shaping the Loch Ness Monster legend.

In Celtic mythology, bodies of water were not merely geographical features but served as a mystical threshold between our world and the 'Otherworld'. These portals were perceived as homes to myriad supernatural beings, including fairies, demons, and water spirits. Among these, the water spirits held a distinguished position, being both feared and respected. Each wave in a river, each ripple on a loch, was attributed to their capricious nature, reflecting their powers, moods, and ancient mysteries.

One of the most notable water spirits in Scottish mythology is the 'Each Uisge', a shapeshifting entity known to take the form of a handsome man on land or a majestic horse near bodies of water. However, beneath this seemingly charming veneer lurked a monstrous water creature known to devour its victims. Then there's the 'Kelpie', a water horse that was believed to lure unsuspecting humans onto its back before dragging them underwater to their doom. Both of these creatures, while intriguing, are also cautionary figures symbolising the treacherous and unpredictable nature of water bodies.

Although the Each Uisge and the Kelpie differ in their descriptions from the popular image of the Loch Ness Monster, their influence is undeniable. They demonstrate an age-old tradition of attributing strange occurrences around bodies of water to the presence of unusual creatures, setting a perfect stage for the emergence of a legend like the Loch Ness Monster. Moreover, their shape-shifting abilities echo in the Nessie tales, where descriptions of the beast often vary, hinting at the creature's potential ability to alter its form.

The waters of Loch Ness have also been linked to 'water dragons' or 'sea serpents', a common creature in Celtic folklore. Known as 'peistes' in Scottish Gaelic, these creatures were often depicted as large, fearsome beasts that lurked beneath the water's surface. They bore a striking resemblance to our modern conception of Nessie, suggesting that these ancient stories could be the precursor to the Loch Ness Monster legend we know today.

In exploring these traditional tales, it becomes clear that the seeds of the Loch Ness Monster legend were sown centuries before the first modern sighting. The mythos surrounding Nessie cannot be extricated from these older beliefs; instead, it is steeped in the lore of water spirits and mythical creatures from

Celtic and Scottish folklore. These narratives have intertwined with the centuries, shaping how we perceive, engage, and wonder about the unknown in the Loch Ness.

The Loch Ness Monster, as we know it, is not merely a creature of the 20th century. Its roots stretch back to ancient times, immersed in the cultural memory of the Celtic people. And like the deep, dark waters of the loch, these ancient stories remain full of mystery, echoing the question: what really lurks in the depths of Loch Ness?

1.2 Ripple Effects - From Ancient Lore to Modern Myth

AS WE TRAVERSE THE foggy landscape of Scottish folklore to the clearer outlines of modern history, we notice how the mythical water creatures have paved the way for the Loch Ness Monster. In this chapter, we'll look at the early historical accounts and legends associated with Nessie, juxtaposing them against their ancient mythical counterparts to discern their similarities and differences.

Let's journey back to the 7th century when, in the biography of Saint Columba, we stumble upon the first recorded mention of a monster in Loch Ness. According to the account by Adomnán, the Irish monk who authored the 'Life of Saint Columba', the saint encountered a beast in the River Ness. Columba intervened as the creature was about to attack a man swimming in the river, invoking the name of God to drive the beast away. Interestingly, Adomnán describes the creature as a 'water beast' rather than a 'water horse', suggesting a divergence from traditional Celtic water spirits.

Fast-forward to the 1930s, when the Loch Ness Monster morphed from regional folklore into a global phenomenon. The infamous "Surgeon's Photograph", allegedly taken by Robert Kenneth Wilson, depicted a head and neck rising from the water, closely resembling the serpentine sea monsters of Celtic lore. This image, combined with numerous eyewitness accounts of a large creature in Loch Ness, breathed new life into the ancient legends, solidifying the image of the Loch Ness Monster as we know it today.

So, how do these early accounts compare with the creatures of Scottish folklore? Let's first consider their similarities. The physical descriptions across the accounts—whether it's the Peistes of Celtic folklore, the monster confronted by Saint Columba, or the modern-day Nessie—all center around a large aquatic creature. The fear and awe they evoke also tie them together. They embody the unknown and the dangerous, representing the unpredictable and powerful nature of water.

However, the differences are equally striking. The ancient water spirits such as the Each Uisge and the Kelpie were not merely creatures of terror; they were also figures of seduction, using their shape-shifting abilities to deceive humans. By contrast, Nessie has remained consistently non-human in form in the eyewitness accounts, and her interactions with humans are mostly passive, without the malicious intent associated with the ancient spirits.

Moreover, the narrative purpose of the legends has also evolved. While the stories of Each Uisge and Kelpie served as cautionary tales against the treachery of unfamiliar humans and the danger of water bodies, the Loch Ness Monster represents the enduring human curiosity for the unknown and the unexplored. The more we search for Nessie, the more she eludes us, feeding our fascination for the elusive and the mysterious.

Through this lens, the Loch Ness Monster can be viewed as an evolution of ancient water spirits—a modern embodiment of the mysteries that bodies of water have symbolised throughout human history. From the cautionary tales of water spirits to the thrill of a cryptid hunt, the narrative of Loch Ness is a testament to how our relationship with nature has evolved, how it continues to inspire wonder, and how, perhaps, we still yearn for a touch of the mystical in our increasingly rational world.

1.3 Beyond the Loch - Nessie in Popular Culture

THE LOCH NESS MONSTER, affectionately known as Nessie, has swum far beyond the boundaries of the Scottish Highlands and into the mainstream of global popular culture. From literature and films to music and even video games, the iconic creature has become a cultural phenomenon, capturing imaginations with its elusive charm and air of mystery. In this chapter, we explore Nessie's cultural significance and its representation across various forms of media.

Nessie's debut into the world of literature traces back to the early days of the monster's popularity. Books like 'The Loch Ness

Monster and Others' by Rupert Gould (1934) capitalised on the public fascination, delving into the evidence and possible explanations. But the creature's reach was not limited to non-fiction; it found a place in fiction as well, permeating children's literature, adventure novels, and even romance. In Stephen King's 'The Tommyknockers' (1987), a character humorously attributes the Loch Ness Monster to alien activity. These literary appearances reflect our deep-rooted fascination with the unknown, with Nessie embodying the thrill of discovery and the enduring appeal of mystery.

In film and television, the Loch Ness Monster has had diverse portrayals. From the family-friendly animated film 'The Ballad of Nessie' (2011) by Disney, to an episode of the iconic sci-fi series 'Doctor Who' (1975), where Nessie is portrayed as an alien cyborg, the creature has been a source of both wonder and entertainment. Even more dramatically, the monster features as the harbinger of an apocalypse in 'Beyond Loch Ness' (2008). Such widespread and varied representations underscore the flexibility of the Nessie legend, its adaptability reflecting our diverse human fears and desires.

In music, Nessie has been both a figure of fun and a symbol of enigma. The Scottish band The Real McKenzies' song 'Nessie' (2005) celebrates the legend, while the progressive rock band Marillion used the mystery of the Loch Ness Monster as a metaphor for personal introspection and soul-searching in their song 'Out of this World' (1995).

Nessie has also found its way into the digital world, featuring in video games like 'Tomb Raider III' and 'Scooby-Doo! and

SECRETS OF THE DEEP: THE MYSTERY OF THE LOCH NESS MONSTER

the Spooky Swamp', and being a popular emoji on social media platforms. The creature even has a Google Doodle dedicated to it, further highlighting its mainstream appeal.

What does the enduring popularity of the Loch Ness Monster signify? On one level, it speaks to our collective fascination with the unknown, the unexplained, and the possibility of creatures lurking in the unexplored corners of our world. But on a deeper level, it also reflects our desire for mystery and magic in an increasingly scientific and rational world.

Moreover, the Loch Ness Monster serves as a powerful symbol of Scottish identity, contributing significantly to Scotland's tourism industry. It has become a national icon, its image adorning everything from whisky bottles to tourism brochures. The creature, in its elusiveness and charm, mirrors the romantic allure often associated with Scotland, its highlands, lochs, and rich folklore.

In sum, the Loch Ness Monster, with its myriad appearances across media, stands as a testament to the human appetite for mystery, a symbol of Scottish cultural heritage, and a remarkable phenomenon in global popular culture. As we move forward, one can't help but wonder how this fascinating creature will continue to inspire stories, theories, and explorations in our collective imagination.

Chapter 2: The Search Begins

2.1 The Image that Shook the World - The Surgeon's Photograph

Among the various bits of evidence that purport to prove Nessie's existence, the Surgeon's Photograph stands as arguably the most influential and controversial. Captured by Dr. Robert Kenneth Wilson in 1934, the iconic image has had a lasting impact on public perception of the Loch Ness Monster. However, the debate surrounding its authenticity continues to rage. Let's delve into the mysteries surrounding this photograph and the arguments for and against its legitimacy.

The Surgeon's Photograph is so named because of Dr. Wilson's profession. A respected London gynaecologist, he was reportedly reluctant to have his name associated with the image, lending it an air of credibility. The photograph depicts a creature with a long neck and small head emerging from the choppy waters of Loch Ness. Its striking resemblance to depictions of aquatic dinosaurs, notably the plesiosaur, sparked widespread interest and excitement.

The picture created a sensation when it was published in the Daily Mail on April 21, 1934. Its striking clarity (for the time) and the reputation of the photographer seemingly elevated it above the realm of trickery or fabrication. It fed into the public's fascination with the unexplained and added credence to the eyewitness accounts that had been trickling in since the early 1930s. The Surgeon's Photograph quickly became the definitive image of the Loch Ness Monster and bolstered Nessie's status as a cultural icon.

However, over the years, sceptics have raised questions about the photograph's authenticity. Some noted the lack of ripples around the 'monster', unusual for a large creature moving through water. Others pointed out that the creature in the photo appears smaller than the behemoth described in eyewitness accounts, suggesting that it could be a smaller object floating closer to the camera.

The most damaging blow to the photo's credibility came in 1994 when an investigation by the Sunday Telegraph revealed it to be a hoax. The report drew on a confession from Christian Spurling, a participant in the scam, who admitted on his deathbed that the 'monster' was a toy submarine outfitted with a sculpted head and neck.

This revelation sparked a reevaluation of the Surgeon's Photograph, casting a shadow over the picture that had for decades embodied the mystery of Loch Ness. However, it did little to dampen public fascination with Nessie. If anything, the controversy surrounding the photograph only added to the monster's allure, transforming it from a simple hoax into a symbol of one of the world's most enduring mysteries.

While the photograph's authenticity has been debunked, its impact on the public perception of the Loch Ness Monster cannot be understated. It has seared the image of Nessie into public consciousness, setting the template for how we envision the creature. In the end, the Surgeon's Photograph stands as a testament to the power of an image and the human desire to believe in the extraordinary, the unexplained, and the mythic.

2.2 Pioneers of the Deep - Early Expeditions and Their Pursuit of the Unknown

THE ENDURING LEGEND of the Loch Ness Monster has attracted numerous explorers, scientists, and enthusiasts over the years, each hoping to unveil the mystery shrouded by the loch's dark waters. In this chapter, we'll journey alongside these pioneering individuals, understanding their motivations, methodologies, and the impact they've had on the ongoing pursuit of Nessie.

Among the first to embark on a serious exploration was Rupert Gould, a British naval officer and writer. Intrigued by the early sightings in the 1930s, Gould conducted meticulous research culminating in his book 'The Loch Ness Monster and Others' (1934). His systematic investigation and validation of eyewitness accounts provided a foundation for future studies and sparked widespread public interest in Nessie.

Motivated by a similar fascination, Edward Mountain, a wealthy Scottish businessman, sponsored one of the first extensive surveillances of the loch in 1934. He employed a team of watchers stationed around Loch Ness, armed with cameras, binoculars, and a determination to capture the elusive creature on film. Although the Mountain expedition failed to procure definitive evidence, it was significant in fostering a methodical approach to investigating the Loch Ness mystery.

The desire to uncover Nessie's secret extended beyond Britain's borders. In the 1960s, an American expedition led by Dr. Robert H. Rines embarked on multiple missions armed with sophisticated technology, including sonar and underwater cameras. Their efforts produced intriguing, albeit inconclusive, results, such as sonar contacts with large, moving underwater objects and underwater photographs that some interpreted as depicting a flipper and a body of a large creature.

Despite their varied backgrounds, these early investigators shared a common fascination with the unknown and a willingness to challenge scientific orthodoxy. Their methodologies, while evolving with technology and time, were rooted in patience, perseverance, and a meticulous examination of available evidence. From scrutinising eyewitness accounts and photographs to employing emerging technologies like sonar and underwater imaging, these explorers significantly contributed to the Loch Ness research field.

These investigations also helped shape public perception of Nessie. Each expedition, regardless of its conclusions, added fuel to the public's imagination and curiosity, propelling the myth further into global consciousness. By dedicating time, resources, and scientific methods to the pursuit of the monster, these pioneers legitimised Nessie as a subject worthy of serious inquiry.

These early expeditions demonstrate the human desire to delve into the unknown, to challenge the boundaries of our understanding, and to wrestle with mysteries that elude conventional wisdom. In the case of Loch Ness, it's a testament to how the pursuit of an elusive creature can captivate the minds of individuals from different walks of life, driving them to the same dark, enigmatic waters in search of answers.

2.3 Frames of Intrigue - Visual Evidence and the Loch Ness Enigma

IN THE CEASELESS QUEST for Nessie, visual evidence has played a pivotal role, offering tantalising glimpses into the loch's murky depths. From grainy photographs to intriguing film footage, this chapter evaluates the reliability and credibility of such evidence, and how they've shaped the ongoing investigation of the Loch Ness Monster.

A significant milestone in Loch Ness Monster research is the Dinsdale Film, shot by aeronautical engineer Tim Dinsdale in 1960. Dinsdale, having initially visited Loch Ness as a sceptic, captured a minute-long footage of a hump-like object moving across the water. His film sparked renewed interest in Nessie, given his scientific background and the fact that his footage was considered some of the best evidence at the time.

The British Royal Air Force conducted an analysis of the Dinsdale Film, concluding that the object was "probably animate." This added a layer of credibility to the footage. However, the film, much like its predecessor, the Surgeon's Photograph, has also attracted scepticism. Critics argue the object could be a boat, its size exaggerated due to a mirage effect on the water.

Subsequent years have seen a slew of photographs and videos claiming to capture Nessie. Among the more notable is the Holmes video in 2007, a film showing a mysterious, almost torpedo-like object, moving in the water. Then there's the Apple Maps satellite image from 2014, revealing a shadowy figure beneath the loch's surface. Each new visual evidence rekindles public interest in the Loch Ness Monster, adding another layer to the unfolding mystery.

However, the credibility of these visual proofs is often contentious. Many images are blurry or taken at a distance, leaving ample room for interpretation and doubt. Further, technological advancements have made image manipulation easier, adding an extra layer of scepticism to new evidence. Nonetheless, these images and videos continue to play a crucial role in the Loch Ness narrative, offering tantalising glimpses that keep the legend alive.

Perhaps the most significant impact of this visual evidence is not on proving or disproving Nessie's existence but on sustaining public interest in the creature. Each photograph or video becomes a piece of a grand puzzle, enticing more explorers, scientists, and curious minds to look deeper into the loch's enigmatic waters. They provide the heartbeat of a story that has captured the world's imagination for nearly a century.

So, as we grapple with the uncertainties surrounding the Loch Ness Monster, the visual evidence, in all its controversial glory, serves as a reminder of our enduring fascination with the unknown, the unproven, and the unfathomable mysteries of our world.

25

EDWARD TURNER

Chapter 3: Exploring the Depths

3.1 Sonar Scans and the Deep Dark - Probing the Depths of Loch Ness

As explorers turned to technology to illuminate the mystery of Loch Ness, sonar emerged as a promising tool. This method, used to detect objects underwater through sound waves, seemed the perfect solution to peer into the Loch's depths. This chapter will delve into the utilisation of sonar technology in Nessie investigations, discussing the challenges faced and the limitations of this method in the search for the elusive creature.

The use of sonar in Nessie investigations began in earnest in the 1960s, and it quickly provided some intriguing results. One of the earliest notable sonar contacts was reported by a team led by D. Gordon Tucker, Chair of Electronic and Electrical Engineering at the University of Birmingham in 1968. He detected a large, moving object at a depth of approximately 180 feet. In the 1970s and 80s, Dr. Robert H. Rines' expeditions employed sophisticated sonar technology, producing echoes suggestive of large, moving underwater entities.

Sonar surveys can cover a large area and provide detailed information about the loch's underwater topography and potential objects within it. It can detect the presence of large bodies in the water without requiring clear weather or daylight.

However, the use of sonar technology in Loch Ness has faced significant challenges. The loch's depth, size, and underwater features present considerable obstacles. Its steep sides often create a 'dead zone' where sonar beams are ineffective. Furthermore, layers of peat washed into the loch can create false signals, potentially giving rise to mistaken interpretations.

Another limitation is the interpretation of sonar readings. An object that appears on the sonar could be any number of things - a school of fish, a floating log, or water currents, to name a few. It's also crucial to note that a lack of sonar contact doesn't necessarily disprove the existence of a creature; it may merely imply that Nessie is adept at evading detection or spends significant time in the loch's sonar dead zones.

Moreover, sonar technology is contingent on the creature being in the right place at the right time, adding an element of luck to an already challenging task. As such, while sonar has deepened our understanding of Loch Ness, it has not been able to provide definitive proof of the monster's existence.

Despite these challenges, sonar surveys remain a valuable tool in the ongoing investigation of the Loch Ness Monster. They represent a rational and scientific approach to a mystery often steeped in folklore and anecdotes. Even in the absence of definitive proof, the application of sonar in the search for Nessie underscores our relentless human pursuit of knowledge and our determination to shine a light, or in this case, a sound wave, into the darkest corners of our world.

3.2 Eyes Beneath the Surface - Underwater

Cameras and ROVs in Loch Ness Exploration

DIVING DEEPER INTO the technology-enabled exploration of Loch Ness, we arrive at the deployment of underwater cameras and remotely operated vehicles (ROVs). These tools offer an opportunity to explore the Loch's underwater world in a way human divers can't, bringing back images from depths shrouded in darkness and mystery. In this chapter, we analyse the benefits and drawbacks of these technological aids in the search for Nessie.

Underwater cameras and ROVs have been part of Loch Ness investigations since the 1970s, often deployed in conjunction with sonar scanning. Dr. Robert H. Rines' expeditions in the 70s and 80s made significant use of these tools, resulting in some of the most controversial underwater photographs, including images interpreted by some as Nessie's flipper and body.

The advantage of using underwater cameras and ROVs is apparent: they can venture where humans can't, enduring the loch's harsh, cold, and dark conditions. They provide visual proof, allowing us to examine the loch's underwater environment in detail. Unlike sonar, which requires interpretation of echoes, cameras provide a direct visual representation of the underwater world.

ROVs, in particular, offer increased manoeuvrability, allowing researchers to navigate around underwater obstacles and reach challenging areas. They can also remain submerged for extended periods, offering continuous surveillance that would be impossible for human divers.

However, the use of underwater cameras and ROVs in Loch Ness exploration is not without its difficulties. Much like sonar, these tools are subject to the loch's conditions. The peat-stained waters of Loch Ness significantly reduce visibility, often resulting in unclear, grainy images that can be interpreted in multiple ways.

Equipment malfunction due to the loch's depth and cold temperatures is another challenge. ROVs, although robust, can still encounter difficulties navigating the loch's underwater terrain, potentially becoming entangled or damaged.

Furthermore, capturing clear images of a moving creature is an exacting task. It would require the ROV or camera to be in the right place at the right time, focused on the right spot, much akin to the challenges faced with sonar technology.

Despite these obstacles, the use of underwater cameras and ROVs represents a significant advancement in the investigation of the Loch Ness Monster. They've brought back images that, while controversial, continue to fuel discussions and theories about what lies beneath the loch's surface.

In the grand narrative of the Loch Ness Monster, these tools represent our undying curiosity and unyielding determination to explore the unknown. They are the physical manifestation of our desire to pierce the veil of mystery that has shrouded Loch Ness for centuries.

3.3 Beyond Sight and Sound - The Promise

of DNA Analysis and Environmental Monitoring

AS WE NAVIGATE DEEPER into the scientific exploration of Loch Ness, we arrive at the fascinating intersection of biology, environmental science, and monster hunting. In recent years, investigators have turned to DNA analysis and environmental monitoring techniques in an attempt to cast a new, potentially revealing light on the Loch Ness enigma. This chapter discusses these advanced techniques and their potential role in identifying Loch Ness' elusive inhabitant.

DNA analysis, specifically environmental DNA (eDNA) analysis, has emerged as a promising tool. This technique involves collecting samples of water and then identifying the DNA fragments within, allowing scientists to create a snapshot of the various organisms that inhabit the water body. The potential application of eDNA analysis to Loch Ness research is groundbreaking: if Nessie exists, it would likely leave traces of its DNA in the water.

In 2018, a team of scientists led by Professor Neil Gemmell of the University of Otago, New Zealand, undertook a comprehensive eDNA survey of Loch Ness. The study's aim was to catalogue the loch's biodiversity and potentially detect any unknown DNA sequences that could point to a yet-undiscovered creature.

The advantages of eDNA analysis are numerous. It's non-invasive, does not depend on visually sighting or sonar-detecting the creature, and is capable of identifying a wide range of organisms. If an unknown or unexpected DNA sequence were detected in the loch, it could provide the most compelling evidence yet for Nessie's existence.

However, the application of eDNA analysis is not without its challenges. DNA degrades quickly in water, making the timing of sample collection crucial. The technique also requires rigorous contamination prevention measures during collection and analysis to ensure reliability. Furthermore, even if an unusual DNA sequence were discovered, linking it conclusively to a large unknown creature would be a significant leap.

Environmental monitoring techniques, such as the study of water temperature, current patterns, and seasonal changes, also play a part in Loch Ness research. These investigations help create a more detailed picture of the loch's environment, potentially shedding light on whether it could support a large, unknown creature.

In the story of the Loch Ness Monster, the application of DNA analysis and environmental monitoring symbolises a turning point, marking a shift from sight and sound-based explorations to the molecular level. They embody the convergence of curiosity, technology, and science in our ongoing quest to decode one of the world's most enduring mysteries.

SECRETS OF THE DEEP: THE MYSTERY OF THE LOCH NESS MONSTER

Chapter 4: Eyewitness Accounts

4.1 The Eyes of the Beholder - Eyewitness Accounts of the Loch Ness Monster

The story of the Loch Ness Monster is as much about the people who claim to have seen it as it is about the creature itself. Their narratives are the lifeblood of the legend, keeping it alive across decades and fueling our collective fascination. This chapter presents an analysis of some of the most compelling and detailed eyewitness accounts of Nessie sightings, exploring the patterns among these testimonies and their impact on belief in the monster.

One of the most renowned accounts dates back to 1933 when George Spicer and his wife reported seeing a large creature crossing the road in front of their car near the loch. They described it as having a large body, about 4 feet high and 25 feet long, and a long, narrow neck, slightly thicker than an elephant's trunk. This testimony, widely publicised, played a significant role in shaping the modern image of Nessie.

In 1951, Lachlan Stuart photographed what appeared to be three humps in the water, again suggesting a large creature. A decade later, Tim Dinsdale captured his famous film showing a large object leaving a wake across the calm loch, corroborating previous accounts of a massive, elusive creature.

Common threads weave through these testimonies, contributing to the enduring image of Nessie. Most describe a large creature with a serpentine neck and one or more humps visible above the water. Sightings often occur during calm and still weather, typically in the early morning or late evening. This consistency has lent some credibility to the accounts and has undeniably shaped public perception of the creature.

However, eyewitness testimonies also carry inherent uncertainties. Human memory and perception are subject to error, and eyewitness accounts can be influenced by suggestion, particularly in a place steeped in monster lore like Loch Ness. Moreover, natural phenomena such as boat wakes, bird flocks, or floating logs can be misinterpreted as monster sightings.

Despite these limitations, eyewitness accounts are an integral part of the Loch Ness Monster narrative. They are the human element in the story, adding depth, intrigue, and an element of relatability. While they may not provide scientific evidence of Nessie's existence, they serve to sustain interest and belief in the creature. They represent our human propensity for wonder, our eagerness to believe in the extraordinary, and our enduring fascination with the unexplained.

The testimonies also underscore the intriguing interplay between perception, belief, and reality. Even as science and technology advance in the quest for Nessie, these human stories continue to captivate us, underscoring the indelible role of personal experience in the pursuit of understanding our world.

4.2 Mind over Monster - Psychological

Explanations for Loch Ness Sightings

AS WE WEAVE TOGETHER the complex tapestry of the Loch Ness Monster, the human mind emerges as a critical piece of the puzzle. Our cognitive processes, the way we perceive, interpret, and remember, play a significant role in shaping our experiences and beliefs. In this chapter, we delve into the psychological explanations behind reported Nessie sightings and misidentifications of natural phenomena.

One key element that may explain why individuals report seeing Nessie is known as "pareidolia". This psychological phenomenon involves recognizing patterns, shapes, or familiar images in random or ambiguous visual stimuli. For instance, seeing a face in the clouds or the image of a sea serpent in a wave or ripple on the water's surface could be examples of pareidolia.

Related to this is the power of suggestion. The widespread publicity surrounding Nessie sightings and the entrenched lore of a monster in Loch Ness could prime individuals to interpret ambiguous stimuli as evidence of the creature. In psychology, this is known as "confirmation bias," where we seek out and favour information that aligns with our existing beliefs and expectations.

Another factor at play is the misinterpretation of the size and distance of objects on the water, a phenomenon known as "size-distance invariance". For example, a piece of driftwood or a group of water birds seen from a distance might appear larger or more monstrous than they are, particularly in the low light conditions when many sightings occur.

The role of memory distortion, or how our recollections can change over time, cannot be overlooked either. Eyewitness accounts often rely on recalling an event that happened quickly and unexpectedly. Over time, the details of these events can become exaggerated or distorted, potentially making a mundane event seem more extraordinary in retrospect.

These psychological explanations do not necessarily discount the possibility of a creature residing in Loch Ness. Instead, they provide a lens through which we can understand why there have been so many reported sightings despite a lack of solid scientific evidence. They also serve as a reminder of the complex interplay between our minds and our perception of reality.

The exploration of these cognitive biases and perceptual factors highlights another fascinating aspect of the Loch Ness Monster tale - how deeply human the story is. It reflects not just our fascination with unknown creatures and unexplored depths, but also our cognitive idiosyncrasies, our perceptions, and the power of our minds to shape our interpretation of the world around us.

4.3 Deception and Trickery - Hoaxes and Pranks in the World of the Loch Ness Monster

THE SAGA OF THE LOCH Ness Monster is not only filled with genuine believers, earnest researchers, and curious onlookers. It also harbours pranksters, hoaxers, and those looking to exploit the monster for fame, profit, or just a good laugh. In this chapter, we delve into some of the most notable hoaxes and pranks related to Nessie and investigate the motivations behind them and the potential impact they have on the credibility of Loch Ness Monster research.

One of the most infamous hoaxes in the history of Nessie is the 'Surgeon's Photograph'. Taken by a respected British surgeon, Robert Kenneth Wilson, the image purportedly showing Nessie's head and neck became the iconic representation of the monster. However, decades later, it was revealed to be a fraud, a toy submarine fitted with a sea serpent head. This hoax left a lasting imprint on the Nessie narrative and continues to cast a shadow on the credibility of other evidence and sightings.

Another well-known prank was the 'Loch Ness Muppet', discovered during a 1972 expedition by the Boston-based Academy of Applied Science. Instead of Nessie, they found a 30-foot model of the monster created for the film "The Private Life of Sherlock Holmes". It had been lost in the loch a few years earlier.

Hoaxing can be motivated by various factors. Some hoaxers may be motivated by the desire for fame or financial gain. For others, the intent might be to ridicule or undermine belief in the monster. Some might engage in deception merely for amusement, to stir up controversy, or to create a buzz.

Regardless of motivation, these hoaxes and pranks undeniably impact the credibility of Loch Ness Monster research. Each exposed hoax fosters scepticism, making it harder for genuine research and credible sightings to be taken seriously. They blur the line between fact and fiction, further complicating an already elusive mystery.

Yet, in a strange way, hoaxes and pranks also contribute to the enduring fascination with Nessie. They add a layer of intrigue, a tantalising mix of deception and humour to the narrative, making the story of the Loch Ness Monster as much about human trickery and gullibility as it is about the quest for an unknown creature.

This exploration of hoaxes underlines a profound aspect of the Loch Ness Monster narrative - the interplay between truth and deception, belief and scepticism, and how easily the scales can tip from one to another in our quest to uncover the unknown.

SECRETS OF THE DEEP: THE MYSTERY OF THE LOCH NESS MONSTER

Chapter 5: Cryptozoology and Cryptids

5.1 The Study of Shadows - Cryptozoology and the Pursuit of Hidden Creatures

In the quest to understand the Loch Ness Monster, we find ourselves crossing paths with a fascinating, if controversial, field of study - cryptozoology. Derived from the Greek words 'kryptos' meaning 'hidden', 'zoo' for 'animal', and 'logos' meaning 'study', cryptozoology is the search for and study of creatures whose existence has not been proven by mainstream science. These creatures, known as cryptids, range from Bigfoot to the Chupacabra to, of course, our very own Nessie. In this chapter, we delve into the field of cryptozoology, its criticisms, and its relationship with the Loch Ness Monster investigation.

Cryptozoology often exists on the fringes of mainstream scientific research. Its proponents argue that it is a legitimate avenue for the discovery of new species, pointing to instances where previously unknown or thought-to-be-extinct creatures were discovered, such as the coelacanth or the okapi. To them, the Loch Ness Monster, and other cryptids, represent unexplored frontiers in our understanding of the natural world.

However, the field has met with substantial criticism and scepticism from the wider scientific community. Critics argue that cryptozoology lacks rigorous scientific methodology. They contend that its reliance on anecdotal evidence, like eyewitness accounts and ambiguous photographs, makes it prone to confirmation bias. Sceptics also point out that many alleged cryptids, including Nessie, lack a convincing fossil record or sufficient habitat to support a breeding population.

Moreover, critics argue that cryptozoology's focus on sensational, unproven creatures can distract from the study and conservation of real, often endangered species. These criticisms underscore the tension between cryptozoology and more conventional scientific disciplines.

Nevertheless, the field's relevance to the Loch Ness Monster investigation is undeniable. Cryptozoologists have been some of the most passionate and persistent investigators of the mystery, contributing significantly to the body of research and public interest surrounding Nessie. While their methodologies and conclusions might differ from those of mainstream scientists, their role in keeping the mystery alive cannot be overlooked.

The study of cryptozoology provides a revealing lens through which to view the Loch Ness Monster saga. It encapsulates the tension between belief and scepticism, between the known and the unknown, and between the allure of mystery and the rigour of scientific inquiry. As we journey further into the heart of the Loch Ness enigma, we are reminded that, at its core, it is as much about our human fascination with the unexplored as it is about the creature itself.

5.2 Beasts Beyond Borders - Cryptids of the World and Their Cultural Significance

FROM THE SHADOWY WATERS of Loch Ness to the dense forests of North America and the remote Himalayan mountains, every corner of the world harbours tales of elusive creatures that exist just beyond the reach of scientific discovery. These cryptids, like our beloved Nessie, capture our collective imagination, inspiring awe, curiosity, and sometimes, fear. In this chapter, we journey beyond Loch Ness to explore other legendary creatures from different cultures and compare them with the Loch Ness Monster.

One of the most well-known cryptids is North America's Bigfoot, also known as Sasquatch. These ape-like creatures, said to inhabit the dense forests of the Pacific Northwest, are often described as large, hairy, and bipedal, bearing a strange resemblance to humans. Like Nessie, Bigfoot has a rich history of sightings, blurry photographs, and footprints that maintain its place in popular culture.

Across the Pacific, in the remote Himalayan mountains, lurks the Yeti, or the "Abominable Snowman". Often depicted as a large, ape-like creature, the Yeti is deeply embedded in local folklore and traditions. While different in habitat and appearance, the Yeti shares with Nessie a sense of mystery and intrigue, spurred on by sporadic sightings and ambiguous evidence.

In Scandinavia, tales of the Kraken, a gigantic sea monster, have been part of maritime lore for centuries. Depicted as a colossal squid or octopus-like creature, the Kraken terrorises sailors by dragging whole ships down into the sea's depths. While far more menacing than Nessie, the Kraken evokes the same fascination with the unfathomable depths and the creatures that might dwell within.

Each of these cryptids, including the Loch Ness Monster, represents the unexplored and unknown aspects of our world. They capture our primal fascination with the wilderness and the uncharted depths, the places where the veil between the known and the unknown is thinnest.

Moreover, these creatures often embody cultural or regional identities. Nessie is as much a symbol of Scotland as Bigfoot is of the American wilderness. They reflect a sense of local pride, uniqueness, and mystery that transcends borders. They also serve as powerful draws for tourism, with visitors flocking to these regions in hopes of catching a glimpse of these elusive beings.

Yet, despite their cultural differences and geographical distances, all these cryptids share one common thread - they are creatures of belief, bolstered by folklore, anecdotal evidence, and a collective desire to believe in the extraordinary. In their elusive nature lies a reflection of our human curiosity, our quest for discovery, and our enduring fascination with the mysteries of the natural world.

5.3 The Pull of the Unknown - Folklore, Cultural Beliefs, and the Perpetuation of the Loch Ness Legend

IN OUR EXPLORATION of the Loch Ness Monster, one recurring theme is the profound impact of folklore, cultural beliefs, and our collective fascination with the unknown. The Loch Ness legend, like many other cryptid tales, thrives at the intersection of these elements, which together form a powerful cocktail of intrigue, speculation, and enduring interest. In this chapter, we delve into the psychological and sociological factors that contribute to our enduring fascination with Nessie and other legendary creatures.

Folklore, stories passed down through generations, forms a vital cornerstone of cultural identity. Folk tales about mythical creatures often serve as cautionary tales, moral lessons, or explanations for unexplained phenomena. They also offer a sense of continuity, linking present generations with their ancestors. The Loch Ness Monster, rooted in local folklore and brought to life through contemporary sightings and evidence, forms an integral part of Scottish cultural heritage.

This intersection of folklore and modern accounts also plays into a universal human trait – our fascination with the unknown. The allure of mystery, the thrill of the unexplained, tickles our curiosity and stimulates our imagination. The Loch Ness Monster, hidden within the depths of the loch, epitomises this uncharted territory. The mere possibility of its existence, despite the lack of concrete evidence, is enough to ignite our intrigue.

From a sociological perspective, cryptids like Nessie can serve as social glue, uniting communities and even entire cultures. Shared belief in these creatures can forge a collective identity, foster social cohesion, and stimulate economic activity, especially through tourism. The excitement and community built around Nessie sightings are evidence of this unifying effect.

Psychologically, belief in cryptids can also be a form of wish fulfilment or escapism. In a world increasingly explained and catalogued by science, cryptids offer a respite – a door to a realm where mystery still abounds, where there is still something new and extraordinary to discover. This inclination towards the marvellous is deeply ingrained in our psyche and is partly why stories of cryptids continue to captivate us.

These sociological and psychological dimensions remind us that the Loch Ness Monster story, and the fascination with cryptids in general, is a profoundly human tale. It speaks to our curiosity, our need for wonder, and our longing for connection – with our past, with the natural world, and with each other. Through this lens, the enduring fascination with the Loch Ness Monster and its cryptid kin becomes not just a quest for hidden creatures, but a reflection of our human quest for understanding and meaning in a mysterious universe.

Chapter 6: Explaining the Mystery

6.1 Echoes of a Bygone Era - The Plesiosaur Theory and the Loch Ness Monster

The quest to uncover the identity of the Loch Ness Monster has given rise to numerous theories, some more plausible than others. Among the most popular is the notion that Nessie is a plesiosaur, a type of marine reptile that thrived during the Mesozoic Era, more than 66 million years ago. In this chapter, we delve into the plesiosaur theory, examining its merits, the paleontological evidence, and the criticisms that challenge its plausibility.

The plesiosaur theory owes much of its popularity to the creature's physical characteristics as described by witnesses and depicted in artistic renderings. With a long, slender neck, a small head, and a large body with flippers, the descriptions match the general appearance of known plesiosaur species. This physical congruence has led many to speculate that a population of these prehistoric creatures somehow survived the mass extinction event that wiped out their contemporaries, the dinosaurs, and found a home in the deep, dark waters of Loch Ness.

Paleontological evidence, however, poses significant challenges to the plesiosaur theory. First, there is no fossil record of plesiosaurs in or around Scotland, suggesting they did not inhabit this region. Second, plesiosaurs were marine reptiles that lived in saltwater environments. Loch Ness, being a freshwater lake, would not provide the necessary conditions for a marine species to thrive.

Furthermore, for a breeding population of plesiosaurs to have survived unnoticed until the 20th century, they would have needed a sufficiently large and genetically diverse population. Given the size and nature of Loch Ness, sustaining such a population would be highly unlikely.

Another challenge to the plesiosaur theory lies in their biology. Plesiosaurs, like all known marine reptiles, had to surface to breathe. This would imply frequent sightings, in contrast with the rarity of Nessie appearances. Moreover, the typical depiction of Nessie with its head and neck out of the water is at odds with the anatomy of the plesiosaur. Current understanding suggests that plesiosaurs could not lift their necks above the water surface in a 'swan-like' pose, as often associated with Nessie sightings.

Despite these criticisms, the plesiosaur theory remains a popular explanation for Nessie, likely due to its romantic allure. The thought of a living dinosaur lurking in a Scottish lake is undoubtedly thrilling. It epitomises our fascination with prehistoric creatures and our desire for mystery in a world where much seems already discovered.

Through the lens of the plesiosaur theory, we see once again that the story of the Loch Ness Monster is about more than just a quest for a hidden creature. It's a mirror reflecting our collective fascination with the prehistoric past, the thrill of the unknown, and the allure of the improbable.

6.2 Slithering Shadows - The Giant Eel Hypothesis and Other Biological Explanations for the Loch Ness Monster

AMONG THE VAST ARRAY of theories posited in the quest to identify the Loch Ness Monster, some of the most intriguing rest on solid biological foundations. One such hypothesis suggests that Nessie might be a giant eel, an idea that has gained traction due to several compelling factors. In this chapter, we scrutinise the giant eel hypothesis, examining the scientific evidence that supports it and its compatibility with eyewitness accounts and other data.

The giant eel theory emerged from the frequent sightings of large, serpentine creatures in the loch. Eyewitness descriptions often depict Nessie as a creature with a long, slim body, which aligns more closely with the body shape of an eel than a plesiosaur. Additionally, we know that eels are native to Loch Ness, further lending credence to this hypothesis.

Perhaps the most significant piece of evidence supporting the giant eel theory is the environmental DNA (eDNA) study conducted in 2018. Scientists analysed water samples from various depths throughout the loch, looking for DNA traces left by animals as they moved through the environment. Their findings revealed a significant amount of eel DNA, suggesting that eels are widespread in Loch Ness.

However, these results, while intriguing, do not confirm the presence of giant eels. The eDNA study could not determine the size of the eels in the loch, and while eels of extraordinary size have been reported, they are not common. Moreover, European eels, the species found in Loch Ness, typically do not exceed lengths of 1.5 metres—far smaller than the size attributed to many Nessie sightings.

Apart from the eel hypothesis, other biological theories suggest that Nessie could be a sturgeon, a large, prehistoric-looking fish known for its armoured scales and size. However, sturgeon are not native to Loch Ness, and their behaviour and physical characteristics don't align well with most Nessie reports.

Another theory posits that Nessie could be a large catfish, such as a Wels catfish. While not native to Scotland, these large freshwater fish have been introduced to some UK waters. Yet, like the sturgeon, the physical characteristics and behaviour of catfish make them unlikely candidates for Nessie.

These biological theories, grounded in known fauna, provide plausible explanations for Nessie's identity. Yet, they also underscore the complexity of the Loch Ness Monster mystery. None fully align with the wealth of eyewitness accounts, photographs, sonar contacts, and other data that have accumulated over the decades.

In the end, our exploration of these biological theories reaffirms the enduring enigma of the Loch Ness Monster. They remind us that while science can offer possible explanations, the truth about Nessie remains as elusive as the creature itself.

6.3 Monsters of the Mind - Pareidolia, Mass Hysteria, and the Psychology of Loch Ness Monster Sightings

AS WE DELVE DEEPER into the Loch Ness mystery, our investigation takes us beyond the realm of biology and into the fascinating world of psychology. The sighting of the Loch Ness Monster, like many experiences of the unexplained, may be influenced by various psychological phenomena, such as pareidolia and mass hysteria. In this chapter, we explore these phenomena and their potential relevance to Nessie sightings.

Pareidolia is a psychological phenomenon where the mind perceives a familiar pattern or form, such as a face or a creature, where none actually exists. It's the reason we see animals in cloud formations, faces on the surface of the moon, or the Virgin Mary on a piece of toast. This cognitive quirk is a byproduct of our brain's pattern recognition system, designed to make sense of the world quickly, even if it sometimes jumps to erroneous conclusions.

In the context of Loch Ness Monster sightings, pareidolia could lead observers to interpret ambiguous shapes in the water as the creature, particularly if they are already primed to expect a sighting. The wake of a boat, a floating log, or a group of seals could easily be misconstrued as the serpentine form of Nessie, especially from a distance or in poor light conditions.

Closely tied to pareidolia is the concept of confirmation bias. This is the tendency to search for, interpret, favour, and recall information in a way that confirms our pre-existing beliefs or hypotheses. An individual believing in Nessie may be more likely to interpret ambiguous stimuli as supporting evidence, reinforcing their existing belief.

On a broader scale, mass hysteria, also known as collective delusion, can contribute to the proliferation of sightings. This socio psychological phenomenon occurs when a group of people simultaneously exhibit similar hysterical symptoms, often spurred by fear, rumour, or shared illusions. In the case of Nessie, one highly publicised sighting could potentially trigger a flurry of subsequent sightings, fueled by heightened public awareness and expectation.

While these psychological phenomena might account for some Loch Ness Monster sightings, they do not necessarily debunk the entire legend. Many sightings have been reported by credible, sober individuals who are adamant about what they saw. Additionally, some eyewitness accounts contain detailed, consistent descriptions that are difficult to dismiss as mere illusions or misinterpretations.

The intersection of psychology and the Loch Ness Monster mystery serves as a reminder that, in the search for cryptids, not all evidence is physical. Our perceptions and interpretations of the world around us can be just as crucial in shaping these enduring legends.

SECRETS OF THE DEEP: THE MYSTERY OF THE LOCH NESS MONSTER

Chapter 7: Beyond the Monster

7.1 From Mystery to Money - The Economic Impact and Tourism Industry of the Loch Ness Monster

The legend of the Loch Ness Monster has not only fascinated and mystified generations but has also played a pivotal role in shaping the economy and tourism industry of the surrounding area. In this chapter, we delve into the economic benefits and consequences of Nessie's popularity, exploring how the local community has both embraced and grappled with the commercialization of their legendary resident.

Undoubtedly, Nessie is a veritable cash cow for the local economy. Loch Ness and its surrounding villages have become major tourist destinations, attracting visitors from around the world hoping to catch a glimpse of the elusive creature. This influx of tourists has driven a robust industry comprised of boat tours, souvenir shops, themed restaurants, and the world-renowned Loch Ness Centre and Exhibition.

Additionally, the tale of Nessie has stimulated the local creative economy, inspiring a wide range of artistic works ranging from literature and music to film and visual arts. These cultural products not only contribute to local revenue but also help keep the story of Nessie alive, promoting a sense of community identity and pride.

However, this prosperity has not come without its drawbacks. With popularity comes the pressure of commercialization, and ethical considerations surrounding the Loch Ness Monster's commodification have been raised. Critics argue that the excessive marketing of Nessie borders on exploitation, turning a beloved local legend into little more than a profitable gimmick.

The surging tourism industry has also raised concerns about environmental sustainability. The delicate ecosystems of Loch Ness and the surrounding Scottish Highlands could be threatened by overcrowding, pollution, and habitat disruption, placing native wildlife at risk. Balancing the economic benefits of tourism with the need to preserve the natural beauty and health of the loch is a constant challenge for the community.

Moreover, the commercial success of the Loch Ness Monster could potentially undermine serious scientific investigations into the creature's existence. Critics fear that the media hype and spectacle surrounding Nessie may overshadow or discredit rigorous academic study, further blurring the line between fact and folklore.

Despite these concerns, it is undeniable that the Loch Ness Monster has become an integral part of the local economy and culture. The challenge lies in managing the monster's fame in a manner that respects both the legend and the landscape, honouring the past while looking ahead to a sustainable future.

7.2 Framing Nessie - Media Influence and Sensationalism in the Portrayal of the Loch Ness Monster

THE MEDIA, WITH ITS enormous reach and influence, plays a critical role in shaping public perception of the Loch Ness Monster. From newspapers to television, and now the internet and social media, different platforms have perpetuated, and sometimes complicated, the legend of Nessie. In this chapter, we delve into how media portrayals and sensationalism have impacted public belief in and investigation of the Loch Ness Monster.

Ever since the Surgeon's Photograph hit the headlines in 1934, the media has played a key role in crafting the narrative surrounding the Loch Ness Monster. The image, published by the Daily Mail, captivated the public's imagination, turning what was primarily a local legend into a global phenomenon. It was the media's early coverage that helped to solidify the image of Nessie as a plesiosaur-like creature in the public's mind, an image that persists to this day.

However, the media's role has not always been neutral or constructive. Sensationalism, the use of exciting or shocking stories at the expense of accuracy, has often permeated the coverage of Nessie. Sensational headlines and exaggerated stories designed to sell newspapers or generate clicks have sometimes blurred the line between fact and fiction, further mystifying the legend. In turn, these sensationalistic portrayals can impact the public's belief in the creature, inflating or distorting the reality of sightings and evidence.

On a more positive note, the media has also provided a platform for discussion and debate around Nessie. Documentaries, interviews with experts, and coverage of scientific expeditions have helped to fuel interest in the Loch Ness Monster and encourage a more critical and nuanced understanding of the phenomenon. This media exposure has often prompted public curiosity, leading to a wider acceptance and interest in cryptozoology and the study of unknown creatures.

Moreover, with the advent of social media, the public now has a direct role in the conversation around Nessie. Photos, videos, and personal stories can be shared instantly, allowing for a more interactive and participatory exploration of the legend. However, this also raises new challenges concerning the verification of information and the potential for hoaxes to go viral.

Navigating the media landscape thus becomes a critical aspect of understanding the Loch Ness Monster phenomenon. The media's influence is double-edged; it can both enlighten and mislead, depending on how stories are presented and interpreted.

7.3 Beyond the Legend - Environmental Significance and Conservation of Loch Ness

AS WE CONTINUE OUR exploration of Loch Ness, it's essential to remember that the loch is more than just a home to a legendary monster. It's a complex and delicate ecosystem with immense environmental significance. This chapter looks

SECRETS OF THE DEEP: THE MYSTERY OF THE LOCH NESS MONSTER

beyond the Loch Ness Monster to highlight the challenges and initiatives related to conserving Loch Ness's unique ecology.

Loch Ness, one of the largest and deepest bodies of freshwater in the British Isles, hosts a rich diversity of life. From the trout and salmon that thrive in its waters, to the otters, birds, and bats that populate its shores and skies, Loch Ness is an ecological wonder. Its location in the Scottish Highlands further makes it a vital part of a larger environmental mosaic, connecting mountains, forests, and other lochs.

However, Loch Ness faces numerous conservation challenges. The influx of tourists drawn by the Loch Ness Monster has a notable environmental impact. Pollution from boats, littering, and the strain on local infrastructure threaten the loch's water quality and the health of its aquatic life. Invasive species, too, pose a significant threat. Non-native organisms, such as the North American signal crayfish, could potentially destabilise the ecosystem by outcompeting local species for resources.

Climate change also looms as an overarching concern. Rising temperatures could alter the loch's thermal structure and impact its aquatic biodiversity. Changes in rainfall patterns, due to climate change, could influence water levels and quality, further exacerbating the challenges facing Loch Ness.

In response to these threats, numerous conservation initiatives have been undertaken. Local authorities have implemented stricter waste management regulations and enforced speed limits for boats to reduce water pollution. Awareness campaigns aimed at visitors promote responsible tourism behaviours, such as using designated paths, disposing of waste properly, and keeping a respectful distance from wildlife.

Scientific research is another crucial aspect of conservation efforts. Ongoing monitoring of water quality, species populations, and climate impacts helps to track environmental changes and inform conservation strategies. Recently, genetic monitoring using environmental DNA (eDNA) has become a valuable tool, offering a non-invasive way to assess biodiversity in the loch.

Additionally, local communities, conservation organisations, and government agencies are working together to control invasive species. This collaborative approach involves public education, early detection, and rapid response to prevent or slow the spread of invasive organisms.

The legend of the Loch Ness Monster has brought global attention to Loch Ness, but it's essential to remember the ecological treasures that reside within and around its waters. As we marvel at the mystery of Nessie, we must also appreciate and protect the complex, thriving ecosystem that calls Loch Ness home.

Chapter 8: Reflections and Speculations

8.1 Lessons from the Enigma

The legend of the Loch Ness Monster, transcending the realm of simple folklore, has had a profound influence on various aspects of society, offering us valuable lessons in belief, skepticism, and the quest for the unknown. As we near the end of our exploration, this chapter reflects on the broader insights gleaned from the phenomenon of the Loch Ness Monster.

The enduring fascination with Nessie provides a fascinating case study in the power of belief. Despite the lack of concrete evidence, the belief in the existence of the Loch Ness Monster persists. This is a testament to the human capacity for faith, the power of storytelling, and our collective fascination with mysteries. It underscores our desire to believe in the existence of the extraordinary, the fantastical, and the unknown, even in an age dominated by science and rational thought.

At the same time, the Loch Ness Monster has also been a catalyst for skepticism. The myriad of theories, hoaxes, and controversies surrounding Nessie has prompted us to question, critique, and demand evidence. This skepticism is a vital aspect of scientific inquiry and critical thinking, challenging assumptions and inspiring rigorous investigation. The engagement with the Loch

Ness Monster has, thus, inadvertently fostered a public discourse on the nature and importance of scientific skepticism.

Perhaps one of the most significant societal impacts of the Loch Ness Monster lies in its embodiment of the human pursuit of the unknown. The ongoing quest to uncover the truth about Nessie reflects our innate curiosity and our enduring desire to explore and understand our world. It's a reminder that mystery and wonder are integral parts of the human experience, sparking innovation, discovery, and a deeper appreciation of the natural world.

Moreover, the Loch Ness Monster serves as a powerful symbol of how folklore and myth can interact with society and culture. The monster has left its mark on everything from tourism and economics to popular culture and media, demonstrating the enduring influence and relevance of such legends in shaping societal attitudes and behaviors.

Lastly, the quest for the Loch Ness Monster has underlined the importance of maintaining an ethical balance in our explorations. The potential for exploitation, whether of the legend for commercial gain or of the natural environment in the pursuit of evidence, serves as a reminder of our responsibilities as stewards of both cultural myth and natural heritage.

The Loch Ness Monster, while a seemingly elusive inhabitant of the Scottish Highlands, has resonated far beyond its alleged watery home, offering rich lessons about ourselves and our society. As our investigation of Nessie draws to a close, these reflections serve not as a conclusion but rather a stepping stone into deeper understanding and inquiry.

8.2 The Critical Lens - Approaching Extraordinary Claims with Scepticism and Critical Thinking

AS WE CONTINUE TO NAVIGATE a world rife with extraordinary claims and mysteries, the importance of critical thinking and scepticism cannot be overstated. This final chapter offers tools and techniques for evaluating evidence and conducting objective investigations into unexplained phenomena, using the Loch Ness Monster as a case study.

One of the first principles in approaching any extraordinary claim is the adage from scientist Carl Sagan, who said: "Extraordinary claims require extraordinary evidence." This means that the more unlikely or unusual the claim, the stronger the evidence needs to be to support it. Sightings of an unknown, dinosaur-like creature in Loch Ness certainly qualify as extraordinary, and thus, require compelling and reliable evidence.

Understanding the nature of evidence is essential. Not all evidence is created equal. Anecdotal evidence, such as personal testimonies or eyewitness accounts, while valuable, are prone to human errors like misperception or memory biases. Physical evidence, like photographs or sonar readings, can be more reliable but are subject to interpretation and potential fabrication. The most compelling evidence often comes from rigorous scientific research that can be replicated and scrutinised by others in the field.

Developing good research skills is another critical tool. Understanding how to find, evaluate, and use information can help differentiate between solid research and pseudoscience. Check the credibility of sources, look for peer-reviewed studies, and be aware of potential biases. Remember that not all information on the internet is reliable or accurate.

Another tool is logical reasoning. Be aware of logical fallacies that can distort an argument's validity. For instance, "appeal to popularity" fallacy could be used to argue that since many people believe in the Loch Ness Monster, it must exist. But the number of believers doesn't validate the claim's truth.

Scientific scepticism is a cornerstone of critical thinking. It involves questioning ideas and assertions until reliable evidence is provided. However, it's essential to distinguish it from cynicism. A sceptic questions and seeks evidence, while a cynic simply disbelieves. Scepticism is not about debunking but about the pursuit of truth.

Finally, maintaining an open yet critical mind is crucial. Extraordinary claims stretch our understanding of the world, but they also challenge us to refine our methods of investigation and broaden our perspectives. While we should be wary of accepting such claims at face value, we must also avoid dismissing them outright without thorough investigation.

In the end, the legend of the Loch Ness Monster serves as more than a captivating mystery. It represents our collective journey in understanding the world, reminding us of the need for critical thinking, scepticism, and the relentless pursuit of knowledge.

8.3 Beyond the Depths - The Future of Loch Ness Monster Research and Open Discussions

AS WE CONCLUDE OUR journey through the mystery of the Loch Ness Monster, it is worth noting that the end of one exploration often marks the beginning of another. The legend of Nessie continues to inspire curiosity, debate, and research, leaving us with boundless possibilities for the future. As we look ahead, we invite you, our readers, to participate in this ongoing dialogue, sharing your own theories, experiences, and perspectives on the enduring enigma of the Loch Ness Monster.

The future of Loch Ness Monster research is as deep and intriguing as the loch itself. As technology advances, new tools for exploration and discovery are becoming available. From more sophisticated sonar equipment and underwater drones to advanced DNA analysis techniques, the future holds promising potential for breakthroughs. Could these new tools finally unravel the mystery of Nessie, or will they lead us to more questions than answers?

Moreover, as our understanding of biodiversity and the environment grows, so too does our appreciation of the complexities of ecosystems like Loch Ness. Future research may reveal yet unknown species dwelling in the loch's depths or uncover insights into the impacts of climate change and human activity on this unique ecosystem. What might these discoveries mean for our understanding of the Loch Ness Monster?

We also invite reflection on the broader lessons learned from the Loch Ness Monster phenomenon. How have our personal beliefs and scepticism been challenged or reinforced by the ongoing investigation into Nessie? What does our fascination with the monster tell us about our collective desire to believe in the extraordinary, the unknown, and the unexplainable?

We welcome your participation in this discourse. Share your theories: What do you believe lurks in the depths of Loch Ness, and why? Share your experiences: Have you visited Loch Ness, and did you have a 'Nessie' encounter? Share your perspectives: How do you think the Loch Ness Monster mystery impacts society, culture, and science?

"Secrets of the Deep: The Mystery of the Loch Ness Monster" is as much about the readers and the broader community as it is about the legendary creature itself. The Loch Ness Monster belongs not just to the realm of Scottish folklore, but to the collective imagination of humanity. Its legend transcends borders and generations, inviting each of us to partake in the captivating quest for understanding the mysteries of our world.

Epilogue: Unravelling the Mystery: Key Discoveries, Unanswered Questions, and the Road Ahead

As our exploration of the Loch Ness Monster draws to a close, we find ourselves standing on the shore of a loch filled with revelations, lingering questions, and the promise of uncharted depths yet to explore. This final chapter summarises the key discoveries we've made on our journey, the unanswered questions that continue to intrigue us, and the enduring mysteries that keep the legend of Nessie alive in our collective imagination.

Our journey through the history and mythology of the Loch Ness Monster has led us through ancient Celtic and Scottish folklore, highlighting the potential influence of water spirits and mythical creatures on the creation of the Nessie legend. We have examined the cultural significance of the monster, from the early historical accounts to its enduring popularity in literature, films, and other forms of media.

The investigation into the physical evidence of Nessie, including the notorious Surgeon's Photograph, the Dinsdale Film, and various sonar readings, revealed a complex interplay of fact and fiction, authenticity, and hoax. We encountered pioneers of Loch Ness research, who, with a blend of determination and audacity, sought to illuminate the mystery shrouded in the loch's deep waters.

From the deployment of underwater cameras and remotely operated vehicles to DNA analysis and environmental monitoring techniques, we've seen how technology and scientific methodologies have advanced the field of Loch Ness Monster research. Yet, with every new technological marvel, we also grappled with the challenges and limitations they posed.

As we delved deeper, we found ourselves face to face with compelling eyewitness accounts, psychological explanations for sightings, and the compelling theories about what the Loch Ness Monster could be - from the fanciful plesiosaur to the more plausible giant eel hypothesis.

Simultaneously, we explored the broader context of the Loch Ness Monster, from the field of cryptozoology and its study of hidden creatures, to the economic benefits and tourism industry surrounding the monster, and the media's role in shaping public perception of Nessie.

Yet, despite all these explorations, the essence of the Loch Ness Monster remains elusive. Questions linger: What really lurks in the depths of Loch Ness? Is Nessie a relic from the age of dinosaurs, a giant eel, a figment of our collective imagination, or something else entirely?

As we stand on the cusp of the unknown, it is clear that the enigma of the Loch Ness Monster is far from solved. The allure of the mystery beckons us to continue our exploration, to question, to wonder, and to delve deeper into the depths of the unknown.

SECRETS OF THE DEEP: THE MYSTERY OF THE LOCH NESS MONSTER

The story of Nessie is not just about a mysterious creature lurking in a Scottish loch. It is a testament to our endless curiosity, our capacity for belief and scepticism, and our collective quest to understand our world. As you turn the last page of this book, remember that the search for the Loch Ness Monster is as much a journey within as it is a journey through the dark waters of Loch Ness.

So, carry with you the spirit of exploration and a sense of wonder. Let the enigma of the Loch Ness Monster inspire you to question, to investigate, and to remain endlessly curious about the enduring mysteries of our world. After all, the search for Nessie is far from over, and the loch's depths are waiting to reveal their secrets. Where will your curiosity lead you next?

Don't miss out!

Visit the website below and you can sign up to receive emails whenever Edward Turner publishes a new book. There's no charge and no obligation.

https://books2read.com/r/B-A-SYIZ-SUKLC

BOOKS 2 READ

Connecting independent readers to independent writers.

Also by Edward Turner

Ghosts of Paris: Ten Haunted Places in the City of Love
Appalachian Nightmares: The Top 10 Creepy Creatures of the Mountains
Asia's Top Ten Cryptids: Legends, Sightings, and Theories
Beyond the Shadows: Unlocking the Mystery of Bigfoot
Evil Women in History: Uncovering the Gruesome Crimes of Ten Notorious Female Killers
Ghosts of London: Ten Haunted Places in The City
Ghosts of New York: Ten Haunted Places in The Big Apple
Ghosts of Oregon: The Top 10 Haunted Places You Must Visit
Ghosts of the Stage: Ten Hauntings at the Theatre
Missouri Nightmares: The Top 10 Chilling Legends
Mothman Unleashed: Into the Darkened Skies
North America's Top Ten Cryptids: Legends, Sightings, and Theories
Philly's Phantom Encounters: Exploring the City's Most Haunted Places
Secrets of the Deep: The Mystery of the Loch Ness Monster
Unsolved Mysteries: Delving into the Shadows of Infamous Murders and Enigmatic Killers
Unveiling the Shadows: A Journey into Financial Crimes and Scandals

About the Author

Edward Turner is a renowned author who specializes in exploring the realms of ghosts, the paranormal, and cryptids. With a captivating writing style and an insatiable curiosity for the unknown, Turner has garnered a dedicated following of readers who are captivated by his thrilling and eerie tales.

Born with an innate fascination for the supernatural, Turner has spent decades delving into the depths of paranormal phenomena, unearthing captivating stories and untangling mysteries that lie beyond the veil of the ordinary. His extensive research and meticulous attention to detail have earned him a reputation as a leading authority in the field.

Through his books, Turner expertly weaves together chilling accounts of encounters with ghosts, offering readers a glimpse into the ethereal world that coexists alongside our own. His ability to paint vivid portraits of spectral apparitions and convey the haunting atmosphere of haunted locations has made his works both spine-tingling and thought-provoking.

Turner's exploration of the paranormal doesn't stop at ghosts. He also dives into the fascinating world of cryptids—creatures that defy conventional explanation. His in-depth investigations into legendary creatures such as Bigfoot, the Loch Ness Monster, and the Chupacabra showcase his commitment to shedding light on these enigmatic beings.

With each page, Edward Turner's readers are drawn deeper into the enigmatic and unknown. His unique storytelling ability combined with his meticulous research has made him a sought-after author for those with an insatiable thirst for the supernatural. Whether delving into ghostly encounters or unraveling the mysteries of elusive cryptids, Turner's books offer a spine-chilling and immersive reading experience that leaves readers questioning the boundaries of our reality.

Edward Turner's works have earned critical acclaim and numerous accolades within the paranormal genre. He continues to explore the unexplained, captivating readers with his distinctive narrative style and unwavering dedication to unveiling the mysteries that lie hidden in the shadows.

www.ingramcontent.com/pod-product-compliance
Lightning Source LLC
Chambersburg PA
CBHW061618130726
47996CB00003B/1031